The High Heels Landlord

SECOND EDITION

Cynthia DeLuca

ISBN: 978-1-7326592-9-2

To my husband, Jerry, for always supporting me in whatever I want to do in life.

To my wonderful children, Hunter, Gabrielle, Michelina, and Salvatore. My inspiration for waking every day!

To my Dad, who always taught me I could accomplish whatever I set my mind to. He is truly the smartest, most ethical man I've ever known.

I could not have accomplished a quarter of what I have in my life without them and the rest of my extended family. They have shown me unconditional love and support every day of my life.

Preface to the Second Edition

When I first published "The High Heels Landlord," I had no idea how many women would reach out to tell me that my story inspired them to take control of their financial futures. Your messages, your questions, and your own success stories have been more rewarding than any rental income I've ever collected.

The first edition was born from my desire to share what I'd learned—sometimes the hard way—about building wealth through real estate investing. I wanted to show other women that you don't need to give up your femininity, your family time, or your high heels to become a successful real estate investor. The response was overwhelming, and I'm grateful for every reader who took that leap of faith with me.

But here's the thing about success—it creates a responsibility to give back even more. After hearing from hundreds of readers, I realized that while my story inspired you, you needed more tools to write your own success story. You needed more detail, more guidance, and most importantly, more ways to apply these lessons to your unique situation.

That's why I've completely updated this second edition. I've added more detail to every chapter, sharing strategies and insights I've learned from years of additional investing experience.

Most importantly, I've added reflection sections to every chapter—practical exercises that help you take my experiences and adapt them to your own life, goals, and circumstances. Because while my story might inspire you, your story is the one that matters. These reflection points are designed to help you write that story with confidence and clarity.

Real estate investing isn't just about buying properties—it's about creating the life you want to live. Whether that's financial independence, security for your children, a comfortable retirement, or simply the confidence that comes from knowing you can take care of yourself, real estate can be your vehicle to get there.

I've walked this path in high heels, and I'm still walking it today. My portfolio has grown, my strategies have evolved, and my confidence has soared. But what excites me most is knowing that you're walking this path too, creating your own version of success.

Thank you for making the first edition such a success. Thank you for sharing your stories with me. Thank you for proving that women can build wealth, create independence, and look fabulous while doing it.

Now, let's get to work on the second edition of your financial future. Your high heels are waiting.

With gratitude and excitement for your journey,

Cynthia

P.S. – Remember, you don't have to literally wear high heels to be a High Heels Landlord. You just have to step confidently into your power as an investor and a woman. The rest is up to you.

Introduction

How many times have you thought about enjoying freedom—financial freedom? Sure, there are lots of ways to achieve this, but being a woman creates some unique challenges.

In times past, we've been expected to cook the dinners, clean the house, get the kids ready for school, do the grocery shopping, and handle countless other responsibilities. But we've never been viewed as the financial provider. Could that change?

What if I told you that, as a woman, you can own rental properties and create financial wealth for yourself, your children, and your family? Wouldn't that make you feel more confident, independent, and successful?

What if I told you that owning a rental property could pay for your child's college education? Or fund your retirement? Or support many other aspects of life? You can accomplish *all* of those things with real estate.

Even if you know nothing about it, you've come to the right place. In just a few hours, I can show you how you, too, can be a successful real estate entrepreneur—all while wearing high heels. (Who said only men get to do the dirty work?)

Don't give up your stilettos!

Somehow, women have never been viewed as equals, even though we're living in a time of supposed independence. (Who needs a man, right?) While we haven't come that far yet, that can change.

Yes, a man can read this book and get the same great information, but what about us ladies? We're still paid less on average, receive fewer promotions, and have to prove ourselves every step of the way.

Many of us have chosen the path of letting our husbands provide for the family. I, too, have been in that situation and was very thankful for that time in my life when I could stay home with my kids.

Of course, the downside was that every time I wanted to meet friends for lunch, my husband had to pay for it. Every time I wanted to spend a day at the mall catching sales, it cost him more. When the kids and I went to see a movie, he had to give us the money to go.

Finally, I thought, "Quit mooching! Don't you want to *create* some income while you're doing all these things instead of being totally dependent on someone else?" I repeated this over and over in my head.

Now, ladies, why would we want to put ourselves in that position? I'm sure your husband is great and would never think twice about supporting you financially, but it costs money to live and eat on this earth. Why not chip in?

Plus, this doesn't require a 9-to-5 job, so why not provide a little income *and* have your time too? Have the best of both worlds. It will give you financial independence, and I'm sure your husband would be proud as well!

So how do you gain independence and create income? Keep reading...

Chapter 1
But I Want It!

W hy do we want anything?

When we enter the land of the mall and see those perfect shoes in the window, that little voice in our head says, "Yes, I've got to have those!" But why do we need them?

You have to answer that same question with everything you buy, and for real estate, this is an easy one. There are so many reasons why you should invest in properties, but how do I list them all?

For starters, how about for your kids, for your family, for a tax deduction, for improving your lifestyle, or just to say you own another home? Yes, that's right—your ego! Lots of people buy real estate for their ego, so it's alright to be upfront and say that your ego is a reason.

My first purchase started when I was talking to a co-worker. He was a retired mayor of a small town up north. He had driven through my town a few years before while vacationing and decided to move here and call it home. (Yes, in sunny Central Florida, many people come here to retire.)

He and his wife had purchased a home in a retirement community and gotten to know the area. They found jobs to keep busy—not for the money, but to stay active. Then he decided real estate was his calling, so he went to school and got his real estate license.

Everything was going great, except that his wife was missing their son. He lived in North Carolina, and like many retirees in Florida, they had moved and left their family behind, only to realize they missed them. This made them wonder what the heck they were doing living so far away.

So one summer day, Jack was telling me how his wife had decided they were moving to North Carolina. Now, you're probably thinking, "What does this have to do with buying rental properties?"

Well, they say opportunity knocks, but what they don't tell you is that you also have to listen for it. That day, having a simple conversation, I had no idea how Jack was about to change my life—but I was listening, so a change was definitely on the horizon.

He went on to say there was only one thing holding them back from going. Though he had just started his new career, he could easily do it again in North Carolina. And they had already found someone to buy their house. So what was keeping Jack and his wife from leaving?

Jack said the only holdup was selling this piece of rental property he had just bought. That's when he looked at me and said, "Hey, you should buy it."

I was in my first year of a new real estate career and not exactly rolling in the dough, if you know what I mean. I had been a stay-at-home mom for several years, which didn't exactly classify me as the "provider" of the family.

Getting my own business off the ground meant a lot of expenses going out and little income coming in, so the last thing I needed to do was buy a rental property that I knew nothing about. Yet I knew people who owned rental properties.

They seemed rich. They seemed confident. They seemed to be on top of the world. Who hasn't heard of Donald Trump? I mean, gosh, everyone rich owns real estate!

So who cares that I should have been cautious? I had bills, credit card debt, and kids in daycare—all with little income of my own and a new career costing me money. There were so many reasons not to do this deal, but for some reason, my curiosity took over. My ego took over. My mouth took over. All I remember is saying, "Yeah, I'll take a look at it."

That same day, Jack drove me to the house. He showed me that because he had just purchased it, he didn't have a tenant yet and hadn't done repairs. The house didn't even have air conditioning—in Florida! What was I thinking?

It was going to be a challenge, but I, being an independent woman, said yes. I decided that I'd buy it!

How stupid was I?

I learned a ton from my first property, but as you continue to buy more, you find you know a lot more the second time around. Therefore, I don't recommend my approach to anyone buying their first property. That being said, let me give you some reasons why I still buy these types of properties today.

The first is for my backup plan. Having a backup plan offers me a safety net in case I fall into financial hard times. What would you do if you lost your job or source of income today? Would it ruin your lifestyle? Would you have to adjust the way you live? The way you spend money? It probably would. But if you own a rental property and you fall into financial hard times, you can sell it and make money that way.

Making money in real estate really isn't that hard if you think about it. When you invest in CDs, money market accounts, or even the stock market, you invest the same amount of money that the investment costs. In other words, if you buy $15,000 of stocks, you own $15,000 of stocks today.

Tomorrow it may go up or down, but you still own roughly $15,000 of stocks right this moment. So if you fall into financial hard times and need to sell your investment, you will get your $15,000 back, plus or minus any losses or gains. But in real estate, you leverage other people's money.

For example, let's say you spend $15,000 as a down payment, finance the rest, and have a $150,000 investment. If the market increases 10% a year, you're earning a 10% increase on $150,000, not just on your initial $15,000 investment.

Your return is much greater in real estate. So if you have financial hard times and need to sell that $150,000 house that you've owned for three years with an average of a 10% return, you could sell it in the neighborhood of $199,000 and make almost $50,000 on your small investment of $15,000. Having a backup plan in real estate is a good idea!

Another valuable reason to own real estate is for the monthly cash flow. Let's say you have $100,000 you can invest. You can purchase stocks that pay a dividend, put them in CDs or some other investment, or invest in real estate.

You can even break it up and use it as multiple down payments, purchase multiple properties, and enjoy a positive cash flow every month. What is positive cash flow?

Positive cash flow is when your mortgage and expenses are less than your monthly income from the property, giving you money in your pocket every month! This works well if you have a property that is paid for free and clear, which brings us to our next reason...

Retirement! We all want to retire, but the real question is: how rich do you want to be when that happens? Being the independent women we are, do we really want to rely on Social Security? Scary thought, huh?

So how can you retire with real estate? Buy one property per year for 15 years, put them all on a 15-year mortgage, and once the first is paid off, start paying more on the others so they are paid off quicker too.

After 20 or 25 years, you will have 15 properties, all paid for free and clear by the tenants' payments. That's the best part—the tenant pays the mortgage for you!

Social Security likely isn't going to be enough to provide you with the lifestyle you want. But now you have 15 properties, all paid for, and all providing you with monthly income. That's even better!

Do you have children still in the house? Have you thought about their college education? How will you pay for that? If you're one of the responsible parents who have invested in a college fund for your children, good for you. No, *great* for you!

But if you aren't in the position financially to invest in a college fund for your children—like the position I found myself in—then I have good news for you. There's another way to offset the costs of college. No, I'm not talking about scholarships, even though those are the best way to offset costs. I'm talking about rental properties, of course.

If your child is four years old, you've got 14 years to worry about paying for college. Buy a rental property now, make your payments on a 14-year amortization schedule, and it will be paid for when your child goes to college. Then you have two options.

If your child is lucky enough to get scholarships, use the monthly cash flow to pay for books, food, and living expenses. Or if you have to pay for education as well, sell the house and walk away with enough to pay for a decent four-year degree. So why not buy a house for each kid? Now *that's* what I call a responsible mom.

Have I convinced you yet? Or do you want more? Okay, one more. So maybe you don't have kids. Instead, you have a nest egg set aside for a rainy day and are supporting yourself quite nicely. Even *more* reason to buy a rental property! Why? Uncle Sam.

No matter how much you make in this country, Uncle Sam wants his cut. How do you keep as much as you can in your pocket instead of sending it to the Internal Revenue Service? Deductions.

Here's where you need a good accountant. The more deductions you have, the less you pay in taxes. So if you're lucky enough to be financially secure, then keep as much as you can in your pocket by having a rental property.

There are the "whys" behind owning a rental property, which is important because you need to have a reason to buy to make it worthwhile. And no matter what the reason, it has to be *your* reason. Don't let anyone influence your thoughts.

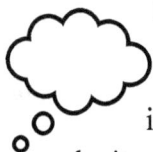

Reflection: Finding Your "Why"

Before you dive headfirst into real estate like I did (remember, I don't recommend my approach!), take a moment to get clear on your own motivations. Your "why" will be what keeps you going when things get challenging—and trust me, they will.

Ask yourself these questions and be brutally honest with your answers:

What's driving you? Is it financial independence? Security for your kids? The desire to stop depending on someone else's income? Or maybe it's that ego boost of saying "I own rental properties." Whatever it is, own it. There's no wrong answer here.

What would happen if you lost your primary income tomorrow? Would you panic? Have to drastically change your lifestyle? Move back in with your parents? If this thought makes you uncomfortable, you're ready to start building that backup plan.

Where do you see yourself in 10, 15, or 20 years? Are you still working the same job, hoping Social Security will cover your bills? Or do you picture yourself with multiple income streams, financially secure, and maybe even helping your kids with their own financial goals?

What's your biggest fear about investing in real estate? Write it down. Is it the money? The responsibility? Not knowing enough? Fear of failure? Once you name it, you can face it and create a plan to overcome it.

What's one small step you could take this week to move closer to your real estate goals? Maybe it's researching your local market, talking to a successful investor, or simply driving through neighborhoods to see what's out there.

Remember, your reason for buying rental property has to be *your* reason. Not your husband's, not your friend's, not mine. When you're clear on your "why," you'll have the motivation to push through the obstacles and make smart decisions— even when that little voice in your head is telling you to buy those perfect shoes in the mall window instead.

Now, let's talk about what happens when other people try to influence those thoughts of yours…

Chapter 2

Advice: Consider the Source

If you've ever been pregnant, no doubt you remember everyone telling you how painful your labor was going to be, the best way to get your baby to sleep, how to handle nursing, and all that other wonderful advice they provided. They meant well, but quite frankly, did we follow all of it? Come on, I didn't even follow everything Dr. Spock said, and my kids turned out fine (I think so, anyway!).

When labor hit, I couldn't remember who gave me advice, what advice they told me, or anything from Lamaze class. I just knew it hurt, and that's all I could focus on! Believe it or not, real estate is kind of like that labor advice.

No, it doesn't hurt that bad, but the similarity lies in the fact that once word gets out that you're interested in real estate, all of a sudden EVERYONE is going to tell you what they think you should do. From "Don't do it!" to "Buy everything you see!" the advice you receive will go from one end of the spectrum to the other.

People who have never even owned investment property will give you advice. People who have never owned their own home will give you advice. Heck, people who still live at home with their parents will give you their advice! So how do you know what (and who) to believe?

When it boils down to that deciding moment, when you're faced with whether or not to buy a rental property, there's only one person in control: you.

Sure, you can try to remember what everyone else told you, or you can choose to take control and focus. You're in control of almost everything in life anyway, and neither labor nor real estate investing is any different.

I know you're probably reading this book thinking, "Yeah, why should I believe you?" Why should you? Because I've lived it and am successfully doing it! No, I don't just own properties for my ego—mine make money, and yours should too. This isn't rocket science. Anyone can do it. But heed what advice you choose to take.

I heard all the same advice stories you will hear. From "You don't have extra money lying around to invest" to "What business does a woman have renting property?" Well, I have a successful business renting property, so there!

Okay, really. The point is that you have to consider the source when it comes to advice. You decide what to file away and never think about again or what to file and keep in the front of your memory.

My first advice came from a gentleman who worked for my dad. Mid was his name. Actually, it was Emidio, but we called him Mid for short. Great guy. Young enough that I could relate to, but old enough to have experience.

Mid was always willing to share information, and real estate was not only his passion—it was his retirement. That was his reason to buy: to retire, and that he did at a very early age.

Now all Mid does is collect rent and enjoy life. Travel and spend time with friends. So what was Mid's advice? "Go for it. What do you have to lose?"

It seemed like such simple advice, sort of like Nike's slogan, "Just do it." But the other part—what do you have to lose? Wow!

Sure, you can lose some money. You can lose your good credit, maybe even put a dent in your ego. But when you compare that to what you have to gain, there is so much to gain!

You gain financial freedom. You gain a "fall back on" investment for a rainy day. You gain the ability to pay for your kid's college. You gain a better retirement. You gain a tax deduction.

There are so many benefits of buying rental property. And even if you really don't need it for any of the above, you could always have it to boost your ego.

Through the years, Mid has helped me more than he knows. In fact, after looking at that property with my co-worker Jack, the first thing I did when I left was go find Mid. And even though we teased him as a "slumlord" because he did weekly rentals, he really knew so much—especially because I didn't know anything!

So I told Mid about the property, and he offered to look at the house with me. It was then when it happened, when he said, "Go for it. What do you have to lose?"

He was right. What did I have to lose? I had a career that was costing me money, nothing in savings, credit card debt, and young children to worry about. I couldn't think of a better time to start investing.

So what's the lesson here? Consider your source for advice. Just as you would with any other aspect of your life, if you're going to take advice from anyone, let it be someone who knows what they're talking about.

Look around at your friends and acquaintances. They'd love to give you advice—trust me on this one. But if you don't have someone in your circle of friends and acquaintances who knows about rentals, read books instead. Lots of them.

Take the advice that makes sense to you and mold it to fit your needs. There are so many books out there that tell you about investing, it's crazy. Just choose cautiously and make sure you take advice from someone who is doing it, not just talking about it!

Reflection: Who's In Your Corner?

Before you make any big decisions about real estate investing, take a hard look at who you're listening to. The voices around you will either lift you up or hold you back—and you need to know the difference.

Who are the people currently giving you advice about money and investing? Write down their names. Now, honestly assess each one: Do they have the financial success you want? Are they actually doing what they're advising you to do? Or are they just repeating things they heard somewhere else?

What fears are people projecting onto you? When someone says "Don't do it!" or "It's too risky," ask yourself: Are they speaking from experience, or from their own fears and limitations? Sometimes the people closest to us try to keep us "safe" by keeping us small.

Who is your "Mid"? Look for someone who is successfully doing what you want to do. This might be someone in your current circle, or you might need to seek out new mentors through books, podcasts, or real estate investment groups. If you don't have a "Mid" yet, make finding one a priority.

What advice have you been holding onto that doesn't serve you? Maybe it's "women shouldn't take financial risks" or "you need a lot of money to start investing." Write down these limiting beliefs and challenge them. Where did they come from? Are they actually true?

What's the worst that could realistically happen if you tried? And then ask: What's the worst that could happen if you don't try at all? Sometimes the biggest risk is not taking any risk at all.

Remember, when it comes to your financial future, you're the one who has to live with the consequences of your decisions—not the people giving you advice. Choose your advisors as carefully as you'd choose your investments.

Chapter 3

Throw All the Formulas out the Window

The good thing about advice is that it enables you to learn a lot from other people's mistakes, experiences, and knowledge. The bad thing is you'll get lots of conflicting information, which can confuse you.

For instance, everyone has a different method of deciding if a property makes money or not. Sounds crazy, but people have varying opinions about making money on their property.

Some think that if a property costs them money over a period of a few years, then they sell it and make $5,000, they've made money. But they neglect to consider all the money they've put into it during their ownership.

Others think that if they buy it and it "breaks even"—meaning that the tenant is only paying enough to cover the rent—then they are making money. But they also neglect to consider all the money they will have to put into the property during their ownership, just for upkeep and normal wear and tear.

With different theories of making money come different formulas for buying properties. Let me give you an example. When you see a house for sale for $150,000, some say that you should be able to rent it for $1,500 a month. This is the 1% theory and probably the most common I've heard.

So with this theory, anything you find that you can make 1% of the cost of the property back on the monthly rent is a good buy. But let's dive deeper into this.

First, this theory doesn't take into consideration property taxes, the amount of which varies from region to region. For example, a $250,000 house in Valdosta, Georgia, is going to have a different property tax bill than one in Phoenix, Arizona. This means that you need to know the exact tax rate for that area before you can figure out how much extra it's going to cost you per year.

It also doesn't take into consideration how much your mortgage payment is. For example, if you put 10% down on a $250,000 purchase and finance the rest at 7% interest for 30 years, your payment will be $1,497, not including taxes and insurance. However, if you put 50% down, that principal payment drops to $832.

Another factor to consider is the amortization length, or how long your mortgage is. Most are 30 years, although you can do less, like 15 years. I suggest you always do a 30-year loan. That way your payment is smaller and more manageable. Plus, it will help you cash flow easier.

That being said, if you remember, I don't recommend that you take the entire 30 years to pay the loan off. In other words, get a 30-year length on your loan, but create your own amortization length to shorten the payoff period.

For example, let's say you get a 30-year mortgage on a $350,000 house at 7% interest with 10% down. Your required principal and interest payment will be $2,096, but you want to pay it off in 20 years. How do you know what your payment will be? You do an amortization schedule for 20 years. This would change your payment to $2,442, and if you can swing the extra $346 each month, you've shaved 10 years off your payments and $168,327 in interest. Not a bad deal, if you can swing it.

All kinds of great websites can help with this, and many are free. The one I use the most is HSH.com. Another great website that can calculate your payment is BankRate.com. With this site, you can also compare different lenders and what they have to offer while also getting a good feel for the going interest rates at the time.

All you need for these types of online calculators is the original amount financed and your interest rate. Plug those numbers in, along with the length of time (in months) you want to pay it off, and it will calculate what your payment should be. From there, you simply start making that payment amount to your mortgage.

You can also download some great apps that will do these same features. Just look around and see what you can find, as they're changing all the time.

Now listen to me carefully. It's very important when paying above your scheduled payment to note where you want the extra money applied. In your case, you want to apply it to additional principal.

If you don't specifically say that, the lender may apply it toward your next payment or your escrow account, which holds your money paid in for taxes and insurance. These choices will not pay off your loan any earlier, so make sure you mark your extra money as additional principal.

One more thing I'd like to mention is that once you make the payment—even if it's above your scheduled payment—you can't get it back. Even if you run into a financial situation and need money, you can't get your additional payments back, so make sure what you pay in, you can afford.

Reflection: Do the Math That Matters

Before you get caught up in all the different formulas and theories floating around, it's time to crunch some numbers that actually make sense for YOUR situation.

What's your local market really like? Don't rely on generic formulas like the 1% rule. Research actual rental rates in your area. Look at similar properties and see what they're renting for. What are the property taxes in your specific neighborhood? What about insurance costs?

How much can you realistically put down? Be honest about your financial situation. Can you do 10%, 20%, or more? Run the numbers both ways and see how it affects your monthly payment and cash flow. Remember, more down payment means lower monthly payments but less money in your pocket for other investments.

What's your comfort level with monthly payments? Think about your current budget. How much extra payment can you realistically afford each month without stressing your finances? Don't set yourself up to be house-poor on your investment property.

Have you factored in the "unexpected" expenses? Beyond mortgage, taxes, and insurance, what about repairs, vacancy periods, and maintenance? A good rule of thumb is to set aside at least 10% of your rental income for these inevitable costs.

What's your exit strategy timeline? Do you want this property paid off in 15 years? 20 years? Before your kids go to college? Work backward from that goal to determine what your monthly payments should be.

Are you prepared for the commitment? Remember what I said about extra principal payments—once you send that money, you can't get it back. Make sure you're not overextending yourself just to pay off a property faster.

The bottom line: Don't let someone else's formula determine your financial future. Run YOUR numbers based on YOUR situation and YOUR goals. That's the only math that truly matters.

Chapter 4

Ditch Your Homework?

Alright, I know no one likes to do homework, but just like your teacher told you in school, if you don't do your homework, you will fail! The same is true in real estate. You have to do your homework. Let me say that again: *You have to do your homework.*

Time and time again, I've heard investors say that they can't rent their newly purchased property. When I start asking them questions, I realize that they don't have a clue why they bought the property, how much the property could rent for, what type of tenant will rent the property (I'm not discriminating—just bear with me and I'll explain later), and so many other important considerations about that particular property or location. They don't have a clue.

It's like they sat down to take a test without doing their homework and didn't know the answers, except this didn't involve getting an "A" on a paper—it involved buying real estate. They bought the property, then realized they didn't have the answers to make it cash flow or rent. So homework is essential. But what is the homework you have to do? Let's break it down.

Research the Property

Researching properties can be a very time-consuming process, but it's necessary. It's much easier to find out bad news in the beginning than to make a mistake, purchase a property, and then realize, "Uh-oh, what was I thinking?" So how are you going to research your property?

The first thing you are going to do is look up the public records, which is the county's information regarding the property. You want to find out anything you can about the property.

Are there any code violations against it? Were there improvements made to it that weren't permitted? (In other words, did they do work to the property for which they did not pull a permit and get legal approval for, such as adding an addition, enclosing a garage and turning it into a living room, and things like that.)

Also, when you call the county or the city, they will be able to tell you if there are any unpaid property taxes against the property. In some situations, these can become the responsibility of the buyer purchasing the property, which means that you need to know this information upfront.

To ensure that you are fully informed about the property you are buying, finding out the history is important as well. The county can tell you who previously owned the property, how long they owned it, and what price they purchased it for. But there is also so much information you can find on the internet now with just a simple internet search of property addresses.

History will also sometimes reveal important information, such as whether the owners bought it for much more than they are selling it for now, which means that they're losing money. Knowing this upfront helps you know how to best handle that situation when you make an offer.

Do a Physical Check

The next step is to go take a physical look at the property. When you go to the property, what you're looking for is to see how much it's going to cost for you to make repairs to get it in move-in-ready condition.

Now listen, I don't expect you to make this home look like the Taj Mahal, but I do expect you to make sure the home is in the same condition that you would want it to be in if you were to live in it. Those are my rules. If I'm going to ask someone else to live in my property, I better be prepared to live in it myself.

In fact, circumstances have actually existed where I've lived in my rental properties before, so this rule has paid off. Besides, if you wouldn't live in it, why would you ask anybody else to and pay you money while doing it?

When conducting your physical examination of the property, make sure you've got a clipboard or something with you so you can jot down notes. What you're looking for is:

- Am I going to need a new roof?

- How's the carpet?

- Does it need the floors replaced or have the hardwood floors resurfaced?

- Is the kitchen missing the dishwasher?

- Are the cabinets half-hanging and need to be re-hung with proper brackets?

Note all of the things needed to get it in top-notch condition. Again, not that you want it to be perfect, but you sure want it to be darn close. We're not slumlords. We're out to do this for the long haul, to become financially independent.

Calculating Your Costs

You also need to look and see how much it's going to cost you to repaint the property. Now I understand, if this is your first property, you're walking in and going, "Huh? I don't know how to do all this stuff!"

Well, look at it as if you were going to buy it and live in it. Would you move into the property without repainting it? If the answer is no, then you better figure out how much it's going to cost to repaint.

The best advice I can give you is to go to your home improvement store, go to the paint section, talk to the people there, and say, "Look, I want to repaint a house. This is the square footage and these are the room dimensions. How much is it going to cost me to buy paint? How much paint am I going to need?" And so forth.

They'll give you a rough idea, but if it's going to cost you $150 in paint, you better figure $175. I always, always, always figure a little bit higher than what I feel the true cost is going to be, just in case I run into those hang-ups and need to spend a little bit of extra money on something.

So you're looking at repairs such as painting, carpet, flooring, appliances, and updating the kitchen—any of that type of stuff. And if there are things that need to be done on the outside of the property—like if the yard is overgrown and you've got to get it cut, bush-hogged, or cleaned up, which means hiring a company to come in and fix it—then you need to consider that also.

What I do is write a list and break everything out. For example, I write that I'm going to spend $4,000 on flooring, $2,000 on paint, etc. I include labor expenses in my estimates because I don't want to have to go in there and do all this work myself.

Of course, you're welcome to do all the work yourself, if you'd like. I think that would be fantastic! But sometimes our time available, our schedules, and our children might not always allow that to happen, so I always write my prices as if I am going to pay somebody else to do the work.

Then, if I end up doing the work myself, great—that's a bonus for me. I basically pay myself that money instead, which essentially means that it's going back into the value of the property.

Once your list is complete, add up your expenses. At this point, you can say, "Okay, I'm going to buy this house for X dollars, but it needs Y more dollars' worth of work to get it rent-ready, so I'm truly spending Z amount."

Be sure to include closing costs because whenever you purchase a property, there are fees and expenses involved. For instance, if you get a loan for your property, there are fees you have to pay to the lender. They can include things such as discount points, origination fees, credit report fees, appraisals, and so forth. So you want to check with your lender to ensure you know all the costs.

To recap, you're going to walk in, look around the property, and figure out the expenses. Then you're going to write your little checklist out and say, "Okay, this property is going to cost us this much." The next question is, "How much can we rent it for?" It may surprise you, but the two have nothing to do with each other.

In other words, if you pay $265,000 for a property, which includes the purchase price and whatever you've spent to get it in rent-ready shape, that does not mean you can rent it for $2,650.

Though some people feel like the 1% rule applies when it comes to renting a property, that's not always the case, so you can't rely on this method of computing the rent. Yes, it's simple, it's easy, and it's quick to come up with, but there are other variables you need to consider.

One of those variables is property taxes and insurance. Your property taxes and insurance are going to fluctuate, which means they're going to go up and down based on whatever the economy is doing and the current price index.

So what you're going to do is figure out, if you're getting a loan for $235,000 to buy the property, can you take the money from elsewhere to do the repairs to get it rent-ready? You are also going to figure out your mortgage price based on $235,000, which is going to affect your monthly payment.

You do this using an amortization schedule as I had mentioned earlier. The amortization schedule breaks out what your payment is going to be based on the principal balance that you take the loan out for (which, in our example, is $235,000) and calculate based on the interest rate you're going to get.

The going interest rate may be anywhere from 5 to 12%, depending on your credit and the market at the time. A fantastic website for current interest rates is bankrate.com. It tells you what banks are offering for interest rates on loans.

Again, I like to be conservative, so you're going to "fluff" it. What I mean by "fluffing it" is, if the going interest rate is 6.125%, you are going to estimate it at 6.5% because interest rates are going to go up and down until you lock in a rate. (Yes, it may possibly go down, but it also may possibly go up, so we're going to be both educated and prepared in case it does go up.)

Now, from that amortization schedule, what are payments going to be? Break it down, remembering that this is only your principal and your interest payment. It's not the "whole enchilada" of what your payment is going to be because you still have to add on a couple of other things. One is property taxes.

If you live in a state that has property taxes, you need to include that in your payment. Once you have a pretty good estimate of what you can expect your property taxes to be, divide it by 12 because that's how many months there are in a year. That number is how much you're going to add to the monthly payment every month. For instance, if the property taxes are $4,800 a year, you're going to add $400 a month (4,800 ÷ 12 = 400) to the principal and interest payment.

How do you find out what your property taxes will be? Call the city or the county and tell them where the property is located, and they should be able to help you estimate the property taxes.

Okay, one more thing to consider: You don't know what your final payment is going to be yet because you also need insurance. Insurance is a vital part of any investment, and it's so great that we can invest in real estate and actually insure our liability and our actual investment. You can't do that with stocks and you can't do that with mutual funds, so it's a great advantage to be able to get insurance to cover our rear.

So our first payment calculation involved principal and interest only. That is called a P&I Payment and stands for principal and interest. But when we add the entire payment up to include taxes and insurance, you get what is called a PITI Payment, which stands for principal, interest, taxes, and insurance.

Whoa! I know I've given you a lot of information in the last few paragraphs, but it is all valuable information to make sure you're doing your homework and that you're well-prepared if you choose to move forward and purchase this property.

To go over it again, what you want to do is get your full payment outlined—your principal and interest payment along with your taxes and insurance—so you can say, "My payment is going to be X dollars a month if I buy that house."

If from doing this homework, you determine you can cash flow that amount, that is fantastic! What that means is, when you cash flow, your investment will make more than you need to pay off the PITI payment (which is typically what most investors want), leaving some extra money left over every month to cover repairs and improvements to the property. In this case, you might be looking at a good piece of property.

My Formula for Other Considerations

There are some additional things to look into when you're doing your research, and I have a formula that can help. If you're worried that it may be too complicated, trust me, it's not. You just have to take a step back and look at it.

First, we're going to start with your gross operating income. Your gross operating income says, "How much money can I make a year off this property?"

For example, you may be able to collect $3,000 a month for rent. That's $36,000 if you were fully occupied for the entire year. So your gross operating income, or your potential operating income, is $36,000 because we're looking at annual figures right now.

Next, you're going to take away any potential vacancy. Granted, with a single-family house, you may be occupied all 12 months of the year, but there is a chance that if the tenant moves out, you might be vacant a month or two because you'll have to advertise the property before you can get another one in.

I use a standard 10% vacancy rule for almost all my properties. It seems to work well, and you don't want to lose more than a month's worth of time (which is roughly 10%) being vacant.

So you're going to take 10% off your gross operating income. In our example, out of our $36,000 annual income, we're going to take away $3,600 just in case we are vacant, leaving a balance of $32,400.

Then you have to consider other kinds of operating expenses. These would include things like:

- If you have to pay for pool maintenance

- If you have to pay for lawn maintenance

- If you have to pay for any utilities

Any expenses along these lines are going to be your operating expenses. Keep in mind that this is for the entire year, so 12 months' worth of expenses is what you're going to put on that line.

Then you're going to take off what I call your debt service. Your debt service is basically the debt you have to pay back, whether it is a mortgage to the bank, money borrowed from a credit card, or money borrowed from a family member or some other outside person.

Anybody you had to borrow money from to secure the property, you have to pay back as a debt. That is your debt service. It is your principal and interest payment, subtracting out taxes and insurance, which leaves you with your net operating income.

If you're serious about buying an investment property and you want to hold it long-term, I highly recommend using this formula. It does not take long to calculate and, if you are computer savvy, you (or get your kids to help you) can easily put it into a Microsoft Excel spreadsheet or something similar so it calculates it for you.

Or better yet, you can download my Cash Flow Worksheet at my website shop at CynthiaDeLuca.com. Use the code HHLBook to get it for free.

Then just plug in the annual rent, the debt service, the estimated taxes, and insurance, and it will figure your net operating income automatically for you. Again, what that essentially means is how much money you'll have left at the end of the year in profit on that property.

Remember, these are all estimations, so things can happen. The roof could start leaking, you could have a fire, you could have damage from a tenant—anything along those lines. But this is what's called "doing your homework in advance" and estimating the true expenses that you're likely going to incur throughout the term of the year. It's all part of doing your homework.

If, after all of this, the property looks good on paper, it's probably a sound decision. But don't stop reading the book yet because there are so many other factors to take into consideration (beyond net operating income) that I want to make sure that you're aware of, so keep reading!

Reflection: Your Property Analysis Toolkit

Now that your head is probably spinning with all these numbers and formulas, let's make sure you can actually apply this homework process to a real property. Remember, this isn't just busy work—this homework could save you thousands of dollars and years of headaches.

Have you identified a specific property to analyze? If not, start looking. Drive through neighborhoods, check online listings, or ask local real estate agents. Pick one property—even if you're not ready to buy yet—and use it as your practice case.

What's your research game plan? Make a checklist of the information you need to gather: public records, code violations, property history, tax information. Who will you call first? The county office? The city? Don't just read about doing research—actually pick up the phone and start making calls.

Are you prepared for the physical inspection? Do you have a clipboard, a measuring tape, and a good flashlight? Have you thought about who might come with you—a contractor friend, a handy family member, or someone with construction experience? You don't have to be an expert, but you do need to be thorough.

What's your "would I live here?" standard? Be honest. Are you planning to cut corners and rent out something you wouldn't live in yourself? If so, you're setting yourself up for tenant problems and a damaged reputation. What specific improvements would you insist on before moving in?

Have you built your cost estimation buffer? Remember my rule: if paint costs $150, budget $175. What percentage buffer feels comfortable to you? 10%? 20%? Don't be the investor who runs out of money halfway through renovations.

Can you handle the real numbers? After running through the PITI calculations and the net operating income formula, does this property still make sense? If the numbers don't work on paper, they won't work in real life. Are you prepared to walk away from a property that doesn't cash flow, even if you "love" it?

Your homework isn't just about one property—it's about developing a system you can use over and over again. The more you practice these calculations, the faster you'll get at spotting good deals and avoiding bad ones. So pick a property and start crunching those numbers. Your financial future depends on it.

Chapter 5

Get Your Finances in Order: You CAN Be in Debt!

Most people think that if you want to invest in a real estate property, you have to have all your debts paid off, have money in the bank in case emergencies come up (like vacancies or repairs), and just have leftover cash lying around. That is *not* the case. In fact, I know very, very, *very* few investors in that situation. Most have more debt than they know what to do with, but it's good debt.

Not many people have a primary residence that pays them money, so that truly is not an asset. Sure, we all want to spend a lot of money on a nice house to live in and enjoy, someplace to have our friends over for dinner, but what does your house pay you every month? Do you get an income from it?

Yes, you may get a nice place to live and your family has a secure roof over their heads and maybe some neighbor kids to play with in the street, but what does your house pay you? What does it put in your pocket at the end of every month?

Instead, an asset is investment properties, stocks, bonds, mutual funds, CDs, money markets, and cash in the bank. Those are all assets because they help you grow your money.

Before going into debt to buy real estate as an asset, you need to get your finances in order. What that means is figuring out: Where can you get the money to pay for your real estate investment? There are lots of choices out there, actually.

Traditional Bank Financing

The first involves going to the bank and getting a mortgage for the property. This seems like a no-brainer, but believe it or not, it's not always the easiest way to buy property.

The way this works is you go to your bank, sit with a mortgage broker or lender, and you get a loan. They qualify you based on your credit, but with an investment property, they also qualify you based on what your tenant is going to be paying you.

The problem is, if you're buying a vacant property, you don't have a tenant. That means that they're not going to look at it as an asset, but as a liability against you because you're taking on additional expenses that you are responsible for covering. So you have to qualify to be able to pay for that.

I highly recommend starting with a very minimally priced property. Don't go out and buy a $400,000 house or even a $350,000 house as your first investment. Instead, you want something more affordable, which is selling for lower than the median sales price of homes in your area. For example, if the median price of the homes in your market is $250,000, you should buy something much less than that.

It's a lot easier to rent to someone who can afford a lower monthly payment than to try to find someone who can afford to rent a $400,000 house. This gives you a greater pool of potential tenants, increasing your odds of renting the property out more quickly.

If you don't know what the average sales price is in your market, pick up your phone and call a Realtor®. They would be glad to tell you. And if they don't know, call the local Association of Realtors®. Heck, you can even search for it online.

One reason you may not want to get a loan or mortgage on the property is if you need to do a substantial amount of repairs. By spending the money on repairs after you purchase the property, you have no way of financing those repair costs with the loan. To recoup the money, you would need to refinance, roll the costs back into the loan, and get that money back out, which is what I suggest you do.

The reason you need that money back is to go purchase your second property. Therefore, you want to make sure whatever money you put into a property, you can pull right back out as soon as possible to keep you going when you feel comfortable enough to start looking for your next property.

Real Estate Is Like a Tattoo

Buying real estate, in my mind, is like getting a tattoo. Once you have one, you kinda want another one. And then once you get a second one, you see something else you like and think, "Gosh, I like that one. I think I want that one too."

Before you know it, you have eight tattoos all over your body. Buying real estate is kind of like that. It gets contagious. Therefore, you want to be able to pull your money back out of your investment as soon as possible so you can reinvest it.

If you do get a loan, you have to put down money to purchase the property for a down payment, and you're going to have to put money down for any repairs. All of that is out of pocket, so the concern is getting the money back as soon as possible.

Since getting a loan right upfront may not be the best avenue, if you have another way to purchase it, then go get a mortgage afterward. That may be the best way so you can roll all the money into the mortgage when you finance it.

The Cash Advance Strategy

Another way to purchase would be, of course, cash. You're probably thinking, "Well, no duh. If I had a bunch of cash, I would go buy it, so why would I even need to talk about a mortgage?"

While we don't always have cash at hand, we may have a way of getting it and not know it. For instance, if you played the credit game before and you have credit cards, I would highly recommend that you start thinking in a new direction.

Credit cards, for me, are 100% for emergency funds or for buying properties. I don't use them for anything other than that. What I mean is, I have credit cards that I've never swiped through a machine. The only reason I have them is to take money off of them, deposit it into my account, and go buy a property.

I have bought properties as cheap as $7,500 on credit cards before. Yes, seven thousand, five hundred dollars. We put $40,000 worth of improvements into it but sold it for $75,000, so that was still a pretty substantial profit.

Regardless, if you can get a cash advance, that may be the best option. A lot of credit card companies will directly deposit the money into your checking account.

Whatever you can do to get the lowest interest rate and get the money as soon as you need it, that's the key here. I know how much available credit I have on different credit cards, and some only have a $1,000 limit while others have a limit over $50,000.

Again, I do not use them for my everyday living expenses. The only money I put on them is when I need to purchase a real estate property or when I am doing repairs to that real estate property. I take the money off the credit card, put it in my bank, and go buy the property.

Then, a few months later, after it's all settled and I have a tenant in there with a lease, I go to the bank and say, "I want to finance this property that I own outright." I also explain to the bank that the credit card debt associated with it is for that property.

Sometimes the bank wants to pay the credit cards directly to ensure that I've paid them off, which is fine with me. It saves me some stamps. Other times they just finance it, give me the money at closing, and I turn around and pay off the credit card companies myself.

The benefit of taking this route is that it helps you keep track of how much money you've spent and how much interest you've spent over time when that property was financed by credit cards. Either way though, you have to be strict about this policy. Pay off your credit cards!

Family and Private Financing

Another option for getting money to purchase properties is to start leaning on family members. You know that Uncle Harry you haven't seen in a couple of years? Maybe he'd be interested in doing some business with you.

That's exactly what this is—a business proposition. Not that you need money because you can't pay the bills. Not that you need money because you can't put food on the table. And not because little Susie wants to take dance lessons. This is purely an investment, so everything goes in writing.

You can take out a loan that comes from anywhere—the bank, credit cards, or your next-door neighbor. Either way, it needs to be legit and in writing to spell everything out and make it very clear. (In the end, I pay interest on all of my loans, so I don't care who I'm paying. I'm still paying interest and they're still making money.)

You would be surprised how many people you know might be willing to do this. I know doctors, lawyers, and others who are financially stable who feel very comfortable doing this because you start out in small amounts. You start making the payments, you finance the property a few months later, and you pay them off.

That's when they realize, "Huh, I feel pretty good about that." Then, when the next deal comes along, it makes it much easier to go and ask them if they'd be willing to loan you some money, usually a little more than last time. They already feel comfortable, you've got a track record with them, and off they go.

When I purchased my first property from Jack, I was in credit card debt, I had a job in a new career that was costing me money, and I had kids I put in daycare to go start this career. So, I didn't have a way to go to the bank and say, "Hey look, I qualify for a loan," because I didn't have any money or any income history. Instead, I asked around and found a Realtor® who knew of someone interested in holding private financing. That's what you're looking for.

Private financing is where an individual loans the money to you instead of a bank. You pay them interest in a signed mortgage against the property, and then when you refinance or sell it, they get paid off. They're highly protected, your interest is protected, everything is in writing, and it's clear and legit.

Basically, instead of paying Big Bank USA, you're paying an individual party. They may want to check your credit and see references, but it's a lot less stringent of an approval process than you're going to get by going through a bank or mortgage broker.

The person I used, I met at the property (I had never met him before that day), he looked around with me for about 30 minutes, looked at me, asked me a couple of questions, and agreed to loan me the money. He gave me $54,300.

He knew he was protected because the property I was buying was worth a lot more than that, and he felt like he was secured against the property. If I did not make the payments, he would foreclose on me and get a property that was worth a lot more than what he loaned against it.

It was a win-win for everyone. He was making interest, he would make a profit if he had to take the property back, and I had already made some payments to him toward repaying the loan. It was all a good deal for everyone.

Check around and see if you know anyone who would do the same for you. You would be surprised how many people would love the opportunity.

Reflection: Finding Your Financing Strategy

Now that you know there are multiple ways to finance your first property, it's time to get real about your own financial situation and options. Don't let the lack of a perfect financial picture stop you—let's figure out what you're actually working with.

What's your current debt situation? Make a list of all your debts—credit cards, car loans, student loans, everything. Now separate them into "good debt" (things that help you build wealth) and "bad debt" (things that drain your wallet). Where does your current debt fall?

How much available credit do you have? Go through your credit cards and write down the available credit on each one. Don't look at this as "money to spend"—look at it as potential investment capital. Which cards have the lowest interest rates for cash advances?

Who's in your financial network? Think beyond your immediate family. Do you know any doctors, lawyers, business owners, or retirees who might have extra cash sitting in low-interest savings accounts? These people might be thrilled to earn higher returns by lending to you. Make a list of potential private lenders.

What's your risk tolerance? Be honest— are you comfortable using credit cards to buy property? Can you handle the pressure of knowing you need to refinance within a few months to pay them off? Or would you prefer the slower but safer route of traditional bank financing?

Have you researched your local market? What's the median home price in your area? What should you be looking for as a maximum purchase price for your first investment? Remember, you want a larger pool of potential tenants, which means staying well below that median price.

What's your exit strategy for getting your money back? Whether you use credit cards, private lending, or family money, you need a clear plan for refinancing and pulling your cash back out for the next deal. Have you researched local banks that do investment property loans?

Are you ready to have "the conversation"? If you're considering family or private lending, practice your pitch. This isn't about asking for help—it's about offering a business opportunity. Can you clearly explain how they'll be protected and what return they can expect?

Remember, the goal isn't to find the "perfect" financing solution—it's to find the one that works for your situation right now. Your financing strategy will evolve as you build your portfolio and your track record. The key is to start somewhere.

Chapter 6

To Incorporate or Not to Incorporate?

Why would anybody incorporate? The first reason is to shield you and your family from liability. If you purchase a property as Jane Doe and someone slips and falls on that property and sues the owner for $50,000, they're suing Jane Doe—which is you. This opens them up to everything you have, which means that if your husband has a nice 401(k) that he's been saving up for a long time at work, that has the potential of being involved in a lawsuit.

You don't want them to be able to take away your husband's 401(k) account. You don't want them to take away your kids' college savings accounts, or so many other things you have worked so hard for. That's why you may choose to incorporate, shielding yourself from that kind of liability.

I did want to go to law school but didn't, so here's my disclaimer: *I am not a lawyer, which is why I recommend that you get advice from an attorney if you have questions about incorporating.* But what I can tell you is that when you incorporate, it is a very easy, simple process. You can do it all online and form a corporation in less than two hours. It really is very simple. Or you can have an attorney help you.

What incorporation means is that you own the property in that corporation's name, and everything that runs through that property is owned by the corporation. The rent gets paid to the corporation, which means that you must have a bank account in that corporation's name.

You also have to pay taxes as a corporation, so yes, you are going to file a tax return at the end of the year for your corporation too. You don't have to file 941 forms and all of that other employee paperwork if you're not going to have staff, but you can still pay yourself for owning your investment. In other words, when there's a profit that comes out of it, you can draw it out as an owner's share or an owner's dividend because your company has made a profit.

Why This Matters More Than Ever

The biggest reason for incorporating is to shield you from liability. Unfortunately, in this day and age, lots of people sue. Did you know that the United States has the most attorneys out of any country in the world? We are a sue-happy country. So if someone slips and falls and they sue, they're only going to sue the corporation and get what's in the corporation if you've done it correctly.

Listen, if a lady can get millions of dollars for spilling a hot cup of coffee in her lap, I am sure someone can get money out of you if they slip and fall at your property. Make sure you are protecting yourself, which also means making sure you have the proper insurance coverage too.

The Bottom Line

Incorporating isn't just for big businesses—it's for smart investors who want to protect what they've worked so hard to build. Your real estate investments should make you money, not put everything else you own at risk. While the process might seem intimidating at first, it's one of the most important steps you can take as a serious real estate investor.

Remember, you're not just protecting yourself—you're protecting your family's financial future. That 401(k), those college savings, your primary residence—all of these should be shielded from potential lawsuits related to your investment properties.

Reflection: Building Your Protection Plan

Before you buy your first investment property, you need to think seriously about protecting everything else you've worked for. This isn't about being paranoid—it's about being smart.

What do you have to lose? Make a list of all your assets: your primary home, retirement accounts, savings, investments, vehicles. If someone sued you personally tomorrow, what could they potentially take? Seeing it all written down might be the wake-up call you need.

How comfortable are you with risk? Some people are willing to roll the dice and own properties in their personal name. Others lose sleep over the possibility of a lawsuit. Which type are you? Your comfort level should influence your decision about incorporation.

What's your current insurance situation? Do you have adequate liability coverage on your current properties? Have you talked to your insurance agent about umbrella policies? Sometimes additional insurance can be more cost-effective than incorporation, or you might need both.

Have you consulted with professionals? I'm not a lawyer, and you shouldn't make legal decisions based solely on a real estate book. Have you scheduled consultations with both an attorney and an accountant to discuss your specific situation? What questions do you need to ask them?

What's your long-term plan? If you're planning to buy just one rental property, incorporation might be overkill. But if you're serious about building a real estate portfolio, you need protection from day one. How many properties do you eventually want to own?

Are you prepared for the additional responsibilities? Incorporating means separate bank accounts, separate tax returns, and keeping detailed records. Are you organized enough to handle this, or do you need to hire professionals to help? What's that going to cost you annually?

What type of entity makes sense for you? LLCs, S-Corps, C-Corps—they all have different advantages and disadvantages. Have you researched which structure might work best for your situation and goals?

Don't let the complexity scare you away from protecting yourself, but don't rush into incorporation without understanding what you're getting into. The goal is to build wealth, not create headaches. Make sure your protection strategy supports your investment strategy, not the other way around.

Chapter 7

Have an Exit Strategy

People who plan ahead for the future always have an exit strategy in place before they get into a situation. You may be thinking, "What in the world is an exit strategy?" Well, let me just fill you in and give you some examples.

Let's say you have some free time this afternoon, but your son has a baseball game tonight at 7:30. So you may be thinking, "I could go to the mall right now, but I need to leave by 5:30 in order to get home, make dinner, and get to the baseball field." In this case, your exit strategy when going into the mall involves knowing what time you have to leave.

On the other hand, if you are like me, I do not like to shop very much (except for rental houses), so I like to go into the mall, know what I'm going to get, buy it, and get out. I don't like to stay there all day, unlike some of my friends who could shop for eternity.

Other exit strategies include dying. When we're born, we know at some point in time we're going to have to exit, right? So how are we going to keep ourselves healthy and happy to exit in a long-term manner so we have plenty of time to enjoy our life on this earth before we go see our Heavenly Father?

And when our kids are born, when we're giving birth and we have that small baby in our laps, we know for the next 18 years of our lives, it's going to be crazy! But we also know that there is an "exit" coming at some point, when they leave, move out on their own, and become self-sufficient, supporting individuals in society. So we know that there's an exit strategy for that.

Exit Strategies in Investing

Now, let me put it in more of a perspective for investing. If you've ever bought stocks, if you've ever saved money and put it in a savings account, if you've ever gotten a money market account, you typically know that when you put money aside, you're putting it aside for a reason.

Whether that reason is that you're saving for your kid's college education, saving to buy a boat, saving because you want to buy a new house for yourself to live in and you know that you need a $10,000 down payment in two years, you're going to break it down and say, "This is how much I need to put aside each month." Your exit strategy in real estate is very, very important to know before purchasing the property.

The first question that always comes to mind, the one that I think about before anything else is, "What is my exit strategy?" If I walk into a property and look at it, do I want to own it for retirement? Do I want to buy it, hold it for a year, and then resell it?

Every once in a while, you may want to do that. If the deal is either too good to be true or it's not really in a rental neighborhood, it's a nice place, and you could get a good retail value for selling it, then take the profit from that and put it back into some more investments. Either way, you must have an exit strategy.

So what is your exit strategy? Do you want to buy the property so that when you retire, it is paid for and gives you your monthly income? Do you want to hold it for a year, then sell it so you can take the profit from it, buy another, hold it for a year, sell it, and make a profit from it and go that way, using the money for your income?

Or maybe you want the money for your current cash flow? In other words, do you want it so that every month, you're making a good two or three hundred dollar profit and you need that right now to use monthly—you need that income? What is your exit strategy? Why do you want to buy the property and how long do you want to hold it?

My First Property Lesson

Don't forget, when I bought my first property, I didn't have a clue what an exit strategy was. I really didn't think about it. I just bought it because it sounded like a good idea. You know... what did I have to lose?

Let me tell you something: my husband has tried to get me to sell that property many, many times. But that was my very first investment property—the first property in my life that I owned by myself, which I still own today—so it has sentimental value to it. I bought it all by myself. That's my property. So maybe it's an ego thing, maybe it's a confidence thing, or maybe it's the fact that the property cash flows very well. Either way, he can't get me to sell it. I'm keeping it.

So when I bought that property, I didn't know what an exit strategy was, but I started to develop it after a year or two and realized that I needed to pay a little bit more attention to what I was doing and be serious about it if I wanted to make a decent living doing it.

My Long-Term Strategy

Ultimately, my exit strategy for that property, and for almost all properties I buy, is a long-term hold. You see, in my business, I'm not offered a 401(k) account and I don't have any type of retirement program or pension with my company, so I have to create my own retirement.

I'm doing this with my investment properties. I know how much I want to make each month when I'm in retirement, what I want my monthly salary to be when I decide to retire, and what my properties need to cover that amount.

Currently, I plan on retiring in the year 2030. My husband and I will be at the right ages, so we decided that's our retirement year. So if I'm going to retire then, I need to know how much income I must have at that point because things are going to cost a little bit more, I would imagine, in 2030 with inflation. I need to know what I need to make each month to not have to cut back on anything when I decide to retire.

Once I figured out how much income I'm going to have to make, this told me how many investment properties I'm going to have to own to make that income by the year 2030. Then I broke it out into how many properties I have to buy each year to make that goal.

My process involves buying the properties and paying them off as soon as possible. The quicker I can pay them off (in a reasonable amount of time, still having money aside for repairs and life expectancy issues, which we will get to in another chapter), the quicker I can start paying down another property and another property and another property.

Then, by the time I retire, all of my properties will be paid for free and clear, with no mortgage or debt against them other than the insurance, taxes, and maintenance. At that point, all the money coming in each month will be my monthly salary.

If I'm sick of being a High Heels Landlord by then, I can also sell all the properties and put a big chunk of change in the bank and travel or do whatever I want to do. Either way, that's my retirement.

Maintaining Your Investment

So, if I'm keeping my property for the long haul, I want to make sure I keep up the property. I'm going to replace the roof when it needs to be replaced. I will replace the heating and the air conditioner unit when it needs to be replaced—all those types of things. I am not going to turn my head and ignore it, which is what we call deferred maintenance. That is where you defer maintaining the property, not what we want to do.

Make sure that, whatever your exit strategy is, you know what it is going in and you can accommodate that with your purchase. Hold it for the long-term or sell it in the short-term, whatever you choose to do. Just make sure you know why you bought your investment and when it's time to get out.

The same principle applies in the stock market. When you buy a stock, you think, "How long am I going to hold onto it? When it makes a certain percentage of increase, will I let it go? When am I going to sell it? If it decreases by a certain percentage?"

Lots of investors use these formulas as investment guidelines. Just make sure you have an exit strategy that suits you.

Reflection: Planning Your Financial Future

Before you buy a single property, you need to get crystal clear about why you're doing this and where you're going. Your exit strategy isn't just about individual properties— it's about your entire financial future.

What's your ultimate goal? Are you
building a retirement plan like I am? Do you need
current cash flow to supplement your income? Are
you saving for your kids' college education? Write
down your specific financial goal and put a dollar
amount on it.

When do you need the money? If you're 25
and planning for retirement, you have time for a
long-term strategy. If you're 50 and need to catch
up, you might need a more aggressive approach.
What's your timeline?

How much monthly income do you need?
I calculated exactly what I need to make each
month in retirement. Have you done this math?
Factor in inflation—what costs $3,000 today might
cost $4,000 in 20 years. What will your expenses
realistically be?

How many properties will it take? Once
you know your monthly income goal, you can work
backward. If each property nets you $300 per month
after it's paid off, and you need $3,000 per month,
you need 10 properties. What's your magic number?

What's your acquisition timeline? If you
need 10 properties and you have 15 years until
retirement, that's less than one property per year. If
you have 30 years, you have more flexibility. Can

you realistically buy properties at the pace your plan requires?

Are you prepared for both scenarios? What if your properties appreciate more than expected and you can sell for a big profit? What if the market stays flat and your only return is rental income? Does your strategy work in both situations?

How will you handle the emotional attachment? Like my first property that I refuse to sell, you might get emotionally attached to your investments. Is that going to help or hurt your exit strategy? Are you prepared to sell when the numbers say you should?

What's your maintenance philosophy? If you're holding long-term like I am, you need to budget for major repairs and updates. If you're planning to sell quickly, you might take a different approach. How will your exit strategy affect your property management decisions?

Remember, your exit strategy can evolve as your life changes, but you need to start with a plan. Don't be like me with my first property—know why you're buying before you sign on the dotted line.

Chapter 8

Hire a Realtor®, Become One, or Look on Your Own? (or Maybe All 3!)

Y ou're going to need assistance looking for houses, and I highly recommend that, if this is your first investment property, you hire the expertise of a Realtor®—but not just any Realtor®.

The Realtor® who helped you purchase your primary residence may be a fantastic Realtor®, someone you loved and who kept in communication with you throughout the whole process. But investment properties are a totally different ball game.

For this reason, I recommend finding a Realtor® with experience in investment properties specifically. In fact, I highly, highly recommend using a Realtor® who owns investment properties himself or herself.

They will better understand because they have been through the process. They know how hard it is to find a tenant, how tough it is to get some repairs done, to find financing, or to go through the hoops and challenges of purchasing a property. So find one who has experience.

Should You Become a Realtor® Yourself?

Maybe you want to become one? "Why would I want to become a Realtor®?" you may be wondering. "I'm not interested in selling properties." Well, let me give you one good reason.

I know lots of people who've obtained their real estate license and became Realtors® because they get to search the Multiple Listing Service® (MLS) themselves. They also have access to advanced search tools and real estate databases. With these tools, all properties are available almost instantaneously when they hit the market. Plus, you can log on and search at midnight, 2 AM, 5 AM, 6 PM—anytime that you want.

Compare this to using a Realtor®, which means you have to pick up the phone and call them to see what's new, get the information, see what time they can show you the property, and coordinate a schedule. Not that this is a problem—it just depends on what level of investing you want to do.

Realtors® also get to be their own representative when buying property and can earn the commission themselves, which can help with the down payment. Sometimes this can be several thousand dollars, so it might be an option you want to look into.

Admittedly, becoming a Realtor® is not a cheap option as it's going to cost you some money (a few thousand dollars) to get your real estate license. Then, of course, you'll also have to learn the ins and outs of real estate and how it works.

However, if you are not going to become a Realtor® and sell properties and make a living at it or make a living purchasing your own properties, I would not recommend becoming a Realtor® or getting a real estate license. There are higher standards that you must abide by when you're a real estate licensee and a lot more disclosures that come into play. It's just much easier to not have to deal with that.

Not that you should do anything against the law—we do have ethics, we do have our reputation to keep in mind, and we also want to make sure we uphold our standards. This means that we don't want to do anything unethical, unfair, or anything like that to another property owner or another person involved in the transaction.

Education Without the License

At the very least though, if you're looking to do this as a long-term process of continual investments over your lifetime, I recommend that you take a real estate course so you know the laws and you learn the rules. It will help you realize some of the things to look for along the way.

Besides, it is always good to know the ins and outs of what's legal, what's not legal, what's required, and what's not required. It helps you better understand all about properties, background histories, title insurance, title searches, ownership—all kinds of things like that. So if you have the time and you don't mind spending it in a classroom, I highly recommend that you take a course.

Going It Alone: Online Resources

Another option is to simply look on your own. There are so many options these days that can help you do this. You can go to your local real estate company's websites and look, you can go to Realtor.com, Zillow, Redfin, or all kinds of real estate sites out there. There are tons and tons of them.

Realtor.com has real estate listings throughout the country, so that's probably one of the most thorough and accurate. But it will only get you so far as it primarily contains properties listed with Realtors®. If you want to look above and beyond that, you need to look at some other real estate websites, like Zillow, ForSaleByOwner.com, Facebook Marketplace, and various "We Buy Houses" investor sites.

Social media has also become a huge resource for finding properties. Many investors now use Facebook groups, Instagram, and even TikTok to find deals. Wholesalers and other investors often post properties on these platforms before they hit the traditional market.

The Learning Curve

Again, if this is your first investment, remember how it was when you had your first kid? You thought, "Oh boy, oh boy, oh boy!" Then your second kid comes along and you're like, "Ah, I already know this stuff. It's a piece of cake." It's the same thing with your investment properties. You're learning as you go. So make sure you get someone with expertise. It is highly, highly worth it.

And if you choose to look on your own, that's fine, but I would recommend getting some help when you go to closing to make sure the property is free and clear of all liens. For this reason, I highly recommend using a real estate attorney if you're not going to use a Realtor®.

Reflection: Building Your Property-Hunting Strategy

Now that you know your options for finding properties, it's time to decide what approach makes the most sense for your situation, budget, and investment goals.

What's your current real estate knowledge level? Be honest—are you a complete beginner who needs hand-holding, or do you have some experience with buying and selling properties? Your knowledge level should influence whether you go with an experienced Realtor® or try to go it alone.

How much time can you realistically dedicate to property hunting? Searching for investment properties isn't a once-a-week activity—good deals move fast. Can you check listings daily? Multiple times per day? Or do you need someone else to do the legwork and bring you the best options?

What's your budget for professional help? Realtor® commissions, attorney fees, and real estate education all cost money. What can you afford to spend on professional assistance? Remember, the right help often pays for itself by helping you avoid costly mistakes or find better deals.

Are you planning to buy multiple properties? If you're serious about building a portfolio, getting your real estate license might make sense. But if you're planning to buy just one or two properties, the time and cost investment might not be worth it. What's your long-term plan?

Do you have any real estate connections already? Think about your network—do you know any Realtors®, contractors, property managers, or other investors? Sometimes the best resources come from referrals from people you trust.

What types of properties are you targeting? Different property types require different expertise. Single-family homes, multi-family properties, foreclosures, and fixer-uppers all have their own nuances. Do you need a specialist?

How comfortable are you with technology? Online property searches, virtual tours, and digital document signing are now standard. Are you comfortable navigating these tools, or do you prefer more traditional, in-person approaches?

What's your risk tolerance for going it alone? Buying without professional help can save money but increases the risk of missing important details or making costly errors. How much risk are you comfortable with on your first investment?

Remember, your approach can evolve as you gain experience. Many successful investors start with heavy professional support and gradually become more independent as they learn the ropes. The key is being honest about where you are now and choosing the level of support that gives you confidence to move forward.

Chapter 9

You Want to Buy What?

The other day, I walked into the mall. There, in the store window, were these awesome, fantastic, amazing, beautiful shoes. They were to die for, and they were only $795. (I'm being sarcastic. I would never spend that much on shoes!)

But maybe you would, so you look at them, and you ponder, and you think, "Oh boy, how great would I look walking in with those shoes on? Oh, everybody would think I was fantastic, that I looked great. They're just awesome. They'd make me feel more confident!"

Is that really how you make a good business decision? Secondly, are they a need? Sure, we need shoes to do our day-to-day duties, but do we need $795 shoes? Well, that becomes a little excessive. You have to do the same thing with real estate. There are certain needs and there are certain wants, and you must differentiate between the two.

Understanding Market Needs

For instance, renting a one-bedroom apartment is a lot harder than renting a two-bedroom because, with a two-bedroom, a lot more people can rent it and use it. So you want to make sure you understand what the market needs are—the necessities, the "I won't take anything less than this" properties.

When you start on your home search process, you may be thinking, "Well, do I really need to have a large yard? It would be nice for the tenants to be able to play in the yard with the kids, but do I really need all that space?"

I'm going to tell you right now, the answer is no, because that's just more yard for the tenant to have to mow, to keep up with, to shovel snow out of, and all those types of things. So a large yard isn't always better. There are plenty of other options for recreation.

Other things you may need, though, could include a certain number of bedrooms, a nice kitchen with plenty of room to cook and have family dinners in, etc. Here are some of the wants:

- **A house with a nice walk-in closet.** Maybe you have a pet peeve of never having a big closet, so you think it's important for your tenant to have a large closet. That is a want.

- **A swimming pool is a want.** Sure, it would be nice to have one and families really enjoy swimming pools. Plus, you may think you can get more rent with a swimming pool, but that is a want, not a necessity.

My Personal "Must-Haves"

Keep it to the bare basics of what the necessities are. For example, a necessity that I have in my rental properties (that may not be a necessity of yours, but I require all of my properties to have one) is a dishwasher. Yup, a dishwasher.

Listen, I have a large family and a lot of kids. Therefore, I need a dishwasher. I hate hand-washing dishes and I hate leaving them around to dry. So I don't care if it's a one-bedroom efficiency that I own—I put a dishwasher in it.

I feel that that is a positive thing that tenants need to have the ability to use. Not all of them use their dishwashers, but that is my necessity that a property has to have. If I buy a property that does not have one, I install one. It's just one of my weird quirks.

So you need to write down a list of what your needs are, and then write a list of all of your wants. Keep these lists in mind when we begin talking about your tenants and what type of tenants each property is going to attract. (Again, I'm not being discriminatory. I'm just telling you that different tenants like to live in different types of properties, so we'll get to that.)

Getting Professional Input

Some Realtors® may be able to offer you a checklist of needs and wants that you can look through. That will give you some ideas as far as what types of things you should need and what types of things you should want.

I can tell you when I'm looking at rental properties, some of the pluses are a fenced yard (not a necessity, but it's a nice touch) and updated electrical or plumbing (which might be something you'll require because these are both a big expense and maybe you don't want to have to go in and replace them or fix them up).

Maybe you're in the roofing business, so you don't mind replacing a roof, or maybe your father-in-law is a roofer. That's okay; that would just be a want then, in that you don't mind buying properties that have roof damage.

Learning from Experience

I've bought a property with asbestos and two types of termites (which, in Florida, there are only three). I bought it for a strategically discounted price because no one else would touch it, even though I couldn't get a loan for it because of the asbestos siding. Didn't bother me.

We paid a very minimal fee to a professional company to remove the asbestos, put on new steel siding which has a hundred-year guarantee, and we don't have any problems with that house. It's a no-maintenance property, but not everybody would touch that. That may be something you may or may not want to get into, but especially with your first property, you want to try to keep it as minimal as possible.

Safety and Practical Considerations

So your needs are going to be things like: if there's more than one bathroom and you think that a family or any kind of small children will live in it, you need to have a bathtub, not just a stand-up walk-in shower. Bathtubs are very important for people with babies—we know this, moms!

I think of things like that when I go into properties. Would I feel comfortable with my children sleeping in these bedrooms? In other words, is there any kind of a hazard? If it's a two-story house, you want to think about getting out if there's a fire. Additionally, is there any other kind of danger which you want to try to avoid or steer clear of?

I personally do not buy investment properties that have swimming pools. I live in Florida. We have swimming pools everywhere. But swimming pools are a huge liability to me because almost every day on the news, it's reported that a small child has drowned in a pool because there weren't proper safety gates up or the parent was not paying attention.

I don't want that kind of liability. I also could not live with myself knowing that someone lost their life at one of my properties. So that is my personal needs and wants list. You need to sit down and write up and make a list of your own, or it can even be something that you're going to build as you go when you start looking at houses.

Building Your List

When you walk around, keep a running list with you so you can note every time you think, "Oh, you know what? That house had a huge basement. I don't like the stairs in the basement," or "Maybe I don't want a house with a basement." Things like that.

Add to your list as you go, kind of like a shopping list at Christmas time. You go in the store, there are all kinds of things to choose from, some things you don't want to get, and some things you do. That's what you're doing as you're building your needs and wants list.

Reflection: Creating Your Investment Criteria

Before you start looking at properties, you need to get clear about what you're actually looking for. This isn't about finding your dream home—it's about finding a property that will make you money and attract good tenants.

What are your absolute deal-breakers? Think about things you absolutely will not compromise on. Maybe it's no swimming pools like me, or no properties built before 1950, or nothing that needs a new roof. What would make you walk away immediately?

What safety concerns keep you up at night? Consider liability issues that worry you most. Pools? Steep stairs? Properties near busy roads? Old electrical systems? Your comfort level with risk should influence your criteria.

What's your skill set and network? Are you handy with repairs, or do you know contractors who can help you? If your brother-in-law is an electrician, maybe outdated electrical isn't a big deal. If you don't know anyone in construction, maybe you need move-in-ready properties. What advantages do you have?

Who is your ideal tenant? Are you targeting families with kids (who need bathtubs and fenced yards), young professionals (who want updated kitchens and minimal maintenance), or college students (who need multiple bedrooms)? Your target tenant should influence your property criteria.

What's your maintenance tolerance? Be honest about how much ongoing work you want to deal with. Large yards mean more landscaping. Older properties mean more repairs. Swimming pools mean constant maintenance. What level of involvement do you want?

What's your budget for improvements? Can you afford to add a dishwasher like I do, or do you need properties that already have everything? Factor in not just the purchase price, but the cost to get the property rent-ready according to your standards.

What does your local market demand? Research what tenants in your area actually want. In some markets, dishwashers are standard. In others, they're luxury items. What features help properties rent faster in your area?

How will you track and refine your criteria? As you start looking at properties, you'll discover preferences you didn't know you had. Will you keep a running list on your phone? A notebook? How will you capture these insights?

Start with a basic list, but be prepared to refine it as you gain experience. Your criteria will evolve as you learn what works in your market and what fits your investment style. The key is to start with some guidelines so you don't get overwhelmed by all the options out there.

Chapter 10

Don't be Afraid to Offend

Y ou know how sometimes you say things that, as they're coming out of your mouth, you're thinking, "Oh no, oh no! Get back in here!'"? We call that putting our foot in our mouth, and it happens when we suddenly find ourselves going, "Whoops! Didn't want to hurt anyone's feelings!"

In real estate, that doesn't happen, so do not be afraid to offend. What I mean by that is, do not be afraid to offend others with your offers. For instance, if someone's asking $275,000 for a house, don't be afraid to offer $200,000. Now, I think you should have some justification or merit for making that low offer, or maybe it's just the fact that you want to get a good deal—and that's merit enough.

But don't worry about the fact that someone has owned the house for 20 years and they're in love with it and it's been their residence where they raised their kids and they have an emotional attachment to it. That doesn't matter. You won't be having Sunday dinners with the owners on a regular basis, so their feelings might get hurt momentarily, but you can't afford to make a bad investment.

One bad investment can turn the meaning of investment totally upside down. A positive can quickly become negative, and now your rental property is costing you money instead of making it. This is a crucial part of the process, and you can't worry about offending the owner of the property because, if the cards were turned, they probably wouldn't worry about offending you.

Keeping It Impersonal

If you are the type of person who will still worry about offending the sellers, even though I'm saying that you shouldn't, ask to see the property when the seller is not there. If you never meet them, you won't have any idea who they are, what type of person they are—you won't have a vision of them. They will be imaginary to you, and it's easier to make an investment offer that's lower to someone you've never met and have absolutely no relationship with than someone you can put a face to.

Lastly, remember that making an offer doesn't always mean the seller is going to accept it. So go ahead, make that offer. My Italian husband says it's like throwing pasta against the wall and seeing what sticks. Your offer may get accepted, and it may not. Either way, what do you have to lose?

This is a business transaction, so you have to separate yourself from it. Be fair, be ethical, be all of the things that make us High Heels Landlords, but don't be afraid to offend others with low offers because it's unlikely that you're going to see them at church next Sunday—and price is everything.

Reflection: Separating Emotion from Investment

Making low offers can feel uncomfortable, especially if you're naturally empathetic or worry about hurting people's feelings. But successful investing requires you to think with your head, not your heart.

What's your natural tendency when negotiating? Are you someone who hates conflict and tends to offer close to asking price to avoid awkwardness? Or are you comfortable with tough negotiations? Understanding your personality will help you prepare for this part of the process.

How will you justify your offers to yourself? Before you make a low offer, do your homework. What are comparable properties selling for? How much work does this property need? What would make it a good investment at your price point? Having solid reasoning makes it easier to stand behind your offer.

What's your strategy for staying detached? If meeting sellers makes you too emotional, plan to view properties when they're not there. If hearing their personal stories affects your judgment, ask your Realtor® to handle communications. What boundaries do you need to set?

What's the worst that could happen? They say no. They get offended. They refuse to negotiate. So what? You move on to the next property. Have you really lost anything, or have you just learned that this property wasn't meant for you?

How will you handle rejection? Not every offer will be accepted—in fact, most won't be if you're making strategic low offers. Are you prepared for multiple rejections? Can you view "no" as simply moving you closer to finding the right deal?

What's your backup plan? If your first offer is rejected, do you have a strategy? Will you increase your offer slightly, or will you walk away? Having a plan keeps you from making emotional decisions in the moment.

How will you remember this is business? Sellers are trying to get the highest price possible— you're trying to get the lowest price that makes sense as an investment. Neither of you is being mean; you're both looking out for your own financial interests. How will you keep this perspective?

Remember, every successful real estate investor has made offers that seemed "too low" to someone else. The difference between successful investors and everyone else is that successful investors care more about their financial future than about temporary awkwardness with strangers.

Chapter 11

Price is Everything, Nothing Else Matters

I hate to go back to shopping, but there is a reason why Walmart has been so successful and is the largest single employer in America. Price is everything; nothing else matters. It's also absolutely imperative that the price is right when it comes to purchasing a property.

If you're going to buy a property and you get it for $1,000 or $2,000 more than you really wanted to pay, then hold it over the course of 20 years, it's really not going to make a difference. It's not going to adjust your payment much, and it's not going to adjust the long-term value of the property over your lifetime. But you *cannot* purchase a property for $10,000 more than it's worth or $10,000 more than your formula states. That will throw off all of your numbers.

Even if you pay $1,000 more, how long is it going to take you to recoup that extra thousand dollars in profit? In other words, if you're making $200 a month in profit from your property and you paid $1,000 more than you should have, how long is it going to take? How many months of $200 per month will it take to average back up to that $1,000 that you lost? It's going to take five months (5 months × $200 profit = $1,000). That's five months of profit you could have made that you spent because you overpaid for the property.

Stick to Your Formula

I don't care what anybody tells you—you have to pay what's comfortable for you and what's comfortable in the formula you used to figure out what you want to pay for the property versus the rent that you feel like you can get. Again, I am always conservative, so if you think that the going rate for rent in this type of property is $750, then guess what? You better think you can get $700 for it. Even though you may think, "Well, I could get $750," uh-uh. Don't do it. Don't be tempted. Try to get $700.

Ever been to a flea market? This is where negotiating comes in handy. You want to go in and say, "I don't want to pay that much. I'm scared to pay that much. What happens if something breaks? What happens if something costs more money to fix than I thought it was going to?" It is very important to understand: you *cannot* overpay for a property. You cannot get emotionally attached.

Emotion Is the Enemy

If you get too emotionally attached to a property, you fall in love with it, or you think, "Oh, I just *love* that, it's so cute and so adorable," guess what? You're going to pay too much for the property. When you go and look at investment properties, you are looking at walls, floors, ceilings, roofs, heating and A/C units, appliances, etc. That is it. Who cares if the carpet is your favorite shade of blue that you've always wanted? It doesn't matter; you're not going to live in it. You can't make money that way.

It's like going out and buying stock in Walt Disney World because you love Mickey Mouse. Is that a smart financial investment? Maybe. Maybe not. That's why you have to do your homework. You have to make sure you're buying it for the right price. You have to make sure you're selling it at the right time, just like any other investment. You have to treat it the same.

Don't fall in love and don't overspend. It doesn't matter if it's on a great corner lot; it doesn't matter if the house is the nicest one on the street (that's bad, by the way). Do not pay too much. Price is everything. Everything, everything, everything is determined by the price.

Reflection: Mastering the Mental Game of Pricing

The biggest difference between successful real estate investors and everyone else often comes down to emotional discipline around pricing. This is where many people fail before they even get started.

What triggers your emotional spending? Think about your past purchases—what makes you pay more than you planned? Is it feeling rushed? Falling in love with something? Fear of missing out? Identify your emotional triggers so you can recognize them when looking at properties.

How will you stick to your formula? When you're standing in a beautiful property that feels perfect, it's easy to justify paying more than your numbers support. What systems will you put in place to keep yourself honest? Will you bring a calculator? A trusted advisor? A predetermined maximum offer amount?

What's your conservative buffer? I always estimate rent conservatively—if I think I can get $750, I plan for $700. What's your comfort zone? How much cushion do you need in your numbers to sleep well at night?

How will you handle FOMO (fear of missing out)? There will always be another property. But when you're looking at one that seems perfect, it's hard to remember that. How will you remind yourself that walking away from an overpriced property is a win, not a loss?

What's your negotiation comfort level?
Some people are natural negotiators; others hate conflict. Where do you fall? If negotiating makes you uncomfortable, how will you push through that discomfort to protect your investment?

Who's on your reality-check team?
Sometimes we need others to talk us out of bad decisions. Who in your life can you trust to tell you when you're about to overpay? Your spouse? A mentor? An experienced investor friend?

How will you calculate the true cost of overpaying? Practice the math—if you overpay by $2,000 and your monthly profit is $150, how long will it take to recoup that money? (Answer: 13+ months) Seeing these numbers in black and white makes it easier to walk away.

What mantras will keep you focused?
"Price is everything." "I'm buying an investment, not a home." "There will always be another property." What phrases will you repeat to yourself when you feel tempted to overpay?

Remember, every dollar you overpay today is a dollar that could have been working for you for the next 20+ years. Successful investing isn't about finding the perfect property—it's about finding good properties at great prices.

The High Heels Landlord

Chapter 12

What the Heck are Amenities?

To put it in easy, short form, amenities are anything in a property that adds extra value that another property may not offer. For instance, things like a pool, a fenced-in yard, a security system, or being located in a community or subdivision that offers any kind of bonuses like a workout gym, community center, or gated entrance—all of these are considered amenities.

A finished attic would be an amenity in a property, as would a screened-in porch, a large deck off the back, a big yard to play in, floodlights on the corners of the property, and so on and so forth. These are all amenities that you need to keep in mind when you're looking for properties.

What Makes Your Property Stand Out?

So you walk in and you go, "Yeah, it's a 3-bedroom, 2-bath, just like any other house I've looked at, but what's the difference in this one?" Maybe it has more square footage, even though it may be a similar floor plan. It may be the same neighborhood or builder, but the amenities make a difference. Sometimes you can charge more rent for amenities, but it's not so much about that as it is getting others to choose your property.

Case in point: Have you ever been to the Clinique counter or Estée Lauder counter where they sell makeup? They use amenities to make us buy. Now, they may not call them amenities, but have you ever seen the offers where, if you buy the $45 cleanser for your face, you get a little makeup bag for free? Those are the amenities they are offering to get us to buy, to get us to do it now, to get us to purchase their product.

The Rental Market Competition

It's very similar to renting. If we can offer more amenities than the next-door neighbor who is renting his house for the same price, our property is going to rent first because we have more to offer. In this way, amenities can be very important, so don't overlook them. Again, look at a property as if you were buying it and moving into it yourself. What are some of the things you'd be concerned with?

If it's a house that's the size for a family to move into, think about *your* kids playing in the front yard, think about *your* kids playing in the backyard. What are some of the things that *you'd* want? Whether it is a security system, floodlights outside to see the neighborhood, a gated community, or a safe area of town where there's not a lot of crime— think about these things. Maybe it's close to a bus stop, and because not all people drive, being close to a public transportation area is also important.

Being close to a school so they can walk their children might also be important. Being close to a store, a gas station, a corner market, or a grocery store—all of those things are pluses. So you have to consider all of those as amenities when purchasing and renting out your property.

The Bottom Line on Amenities

You may not pay more for the property (nor should you), it may not make the property more valuable, and you may not be able to get more income when you rent it, but if it puts you one step ahead of the competition, that's what you want because you want your property to rent first.

Reflection: Identifying Your Property's Competitive Advantages

Amenities can be the difference between your property sitting vacant for months and getting rented within days. But not all amenities are created equal, and what matters depends entirely on your target market.

Who is your ideal tenant? Are you targeting young professionals, families with kids, retirees, or college students? A home office setup might be crucial for remote workers, but families might care more about a fenced yard and proximity

The High Heels Landlord

to schools. What does your target tenant actually want?

What amenities are standard in your market? Research your competition. If every rental in your area has a dishwasher, that's not an amenity—it's an expectation. But if you're the only one with a garage or updated appliances, that could be your competitive edge. What's considered basic versus special in your market?

Which amenities actually matter to renters? Some amenities sound great but don't actually influence rental decisions. Others seem minor but are deal-breakers. Have you talked to local property managers or current renters about what they value most? What research have you done?

What's the cost-benefit analysis? Some amenities are expensive to install and maintain (like pools), while others are relatively cheap but high-impact (like good lighting or fresh paint). Which amenities give you the best return on investment in terms of faster rentals or slightly higher rents?

How will you market your amenities? Having great amenities doesn't help if potential tenants don't know about them. How will you highlight these features in your listings, photos, and property showings? What story will you tell about the lifestyle your property offers?

What location-based amenities do you have? Sometimes the best amenities aren't on the property itself—they're in the neighborhood. Proximity to public transportation, good schools, shopping, or entertainment can be huge selling points. What advantages does your property's location offer?

Are you prepared to maintain amenity-related expectations? If you advertise a "beautifully landscaped yard," you need to keep it that way. If you highlight the "updated kitchen," it needs to stay updated. What ongoing commitments are you making with your amenity promises?

How will you stay ahead of the competition? Markets change, and what's considered a luxury amenity today might be standard tomorrow. How will you continue to differentiate your property over time? What's your plan for staying competitive?

Remember, amenities aren't just about the physical features of the property—they're about the lifestyle and convenience you're offering. Think like a renter, not just like an investor, and you'll start to see what really matters in the rental market.

Chapter 13

The Question of Multi-Family Properties

A dear friend came to me the other day and asked me for my advice. He's been my friend for many years and knows that I own real estate properties, so we went to lunch and discussed his option to purchase a property.

It's a one-story, nine-unit residential complex that's almost fully occupied, with only two vacancies out of the nine. But it's also been severely neglected. The owner does hardly anything to communicate with the tenants or get rent paid on time, so it has room for improvement. (Any time you run into a situation where the property is not being managed to its fullest potential, that's an opportunity because it means you can go in there, do a better job, and raise the rent, which is fantastic.)

The Problem with Jumping in Too Deep

In this situation, my friend doesn't own any other real estate investments and never has. As a matter of fact, he still lives in the first property he's ever owned. He does own some land, but he doesn't own any rentals, which means that he's never dealt with tenants, he's never dealt with repairs, and he's never dealt with any other landlord-tenant type of situations.

Based on this, my concern was that it was nine units. He was potentially throwing himself into something that's way over his head, and he didn't have enough education yet. It's kind of like having no kids then, all of a sudden, having nine babies to look after. How would you do it? You wouldn't know how to make bottles for nine kids at the same time, how you would change all nine diapers... I mean, goodness! You'd have to hire a nanny.

In this situation, I felt the same way. He'd have to hire help. He couldn't continue with his full-time job and manage this property too. It would be too much of a workload.

Plus, though I believe in hiring help when you need it, in this situation, my friend didn't know what he was doing. How does he know he's going to hire a manager who's going to be able to take care of the units well? Of course, he knows me, but how else is he going to make sure he's staying on top of things and that he can improve the amount of income coming from the property?

The Case for Multi-Family... Later

When it comes to multi-family properties, I suggest that you do not purchase them as your first property. Once you get some experience under your belt, I believe in multi-family properties as a great investment, and you should make this a goal.

The benefit of having a duplex, which is a two-unit property, means that if one side is vacant, you're still getting some income from the other side. So even though one side isn't making you any money because there isn't a tenant in it, at least you're getting something from the other side to put toward the mortgage payment. You do not have to pay the entire balance yourself, out of your own income.

However, jumping into these properties at the beginning is just a little bit too much. Remember, we don't want to jump into having nine kids at once. Twins? Maybe. But I wouldn't go anything more than that the first time around.

And if you don't believe me, just think about having children. That may convince you otherwise.

Reflection: Assessing Your Readiness for Property Management

Before you get excited about the potential income from multi-unit properties, honestly evaluate whether you're ready for the responsibility that comes with them.

What's your current experience level?
Have you ever been a landlord before? Have you
dealt with tenant issues, late rent, emergency
repairs, or evictions? If you've never managed even
one tenant, managing multiple units simultaneously
could be overwhelming. What preparation do you
need?

**How much time can you realistically
dedicate?** Managing rental properties isn't a passive
investment—it requires time for tenant
communication, maintenance coordination, rent
collection, and problem-solving. With your current
job and family commitments, how many hours per
week can you realistically dedicate to property
management?

What's your support system? Do you have
reliable contractors, a good attorney, an experienced
property manager you could hire, or mentor
investors you can call for advice? If you're going it
alone, you might want to start smaller. Who's in
your corner?

**Can you handle multiple problems at
once?** Single-family properties usually have one
major issue at a time. Multi-unit properties can have
several tenants with problems simultaneously—a
broken air conditioner in unit 3, late rent from unit
7, and a move-out in unit 5, all in the same week.

How well do you handle stress and multiple priorities?

What's your financial cushion? Multi-unit properties can have higher vacancy rates and more expensive repairs. If half your units are vacant, can you cover the mortgage and expenses until they're rented? Do you have enough reserves for major repairs like roof replacement or HVAC systems?

Are you prepared for the learning curve? Every mistake you make as a landlord gets multiplied by the number of units you own. A poor tenant screening process might mean one bad tenant in a single-family home, but it could mean multiple problem tenants in a multi-unit property. Are you ready to learn expensive lessons?

What's your long-term goal? If your goal is to own multiple properties eventually, starting with a single-family home lets you learn the business with lower stakes. If your goal is passive income, you might need to hire management from day one. What are you really trying to achieve?

How will you measure success? With multi-unit properties, success isn't just about positive cash flow—it's about occupancy rates, tenant retention, efficient maintenance, and staying competitive in the market. Do you know how to track and improve these metrics?

Remember, there's no shame in starting small. Every successful real estate investor started with their first property. The goal is to build your skills and confidence so that when you do take on that multi-unit property, you'll be ready to succeed rather than just survive.

Chapter 14

Know Your Tenant Before You Buy

W hat type of tenant is going to be attracted to your property? For example, if you buy a one-bedroom efficiency, do you think a single mother with three children is going to rent that property from you? Probably not, because there's not enough room for everybody to live in it.

And if you're going to buy a 4-bedroom, 2-bathroom, 2,600 square foot home, are you going to have a single person interested in renting it? Probably not. It's probably going to be a large family that rents that sized property from you.

Understanding Your Consumer

So, what I mean by knowing your tenant is: who is going to be your consumer? It's just like when Nissan decides to make a minivan. They build it based on the consumer who they feel is going to purchase it. They consider what age group they're going to be in, what type of family situation they have, etc.

For example, most people who buy minivans have children, so they target that group. Most people who buy minivans also are not single people who drive to and from work five miles a day, and that's it. Usually, those people get small, economical cars.

So, if you're going to buy a large home, you have to consider that you're going to need a large family to fill it, most likely. And if you're going to buy a small home, you have to think that you're cutting out some people who may be able to rent it because the home is too small for them to live in.

Location Influences Your Tenant Pool

Another thing to keep in mind: if you're near a university, college, or technical school, you might get some students who want to rent from you— nothing wrong with that. And if you're near a big interstate or highway that is a good commute route into a larger city for work, consider that you might get some people who commute back and forth from work—that's okay as well.

If you have homes based around a big hospital, a lot of the time you get nurses or doctors who may want to rent from you when they move into the area to transfer to the hospital. Keep in mind what area your property is located in, what it's near, and what size family or individual is typically going to be renting it. Keep in mind who your tenants are before you buy.

The Economics of Tenant Pool Size

For example, if you buy a 4-bedroom house that has 2,600 square feet, not everyone can afford to rent that. Plus, typically when you rent to a family of that size, they might be in the position to buy, so they may not be interested in renting at all. This means that there are a lot fewer people out there you can rent to with this property—a much smaller group.

Alternatively, if you buy a small house, a lot of people starting out in life—either those who are moving out from their parents' house or moving into the area as a job transfer—start with something small and affordable until they can get into a better financial situation where they can move up. So I would highly recommend starting out small.

Do you remember your first house or apartment? It probably wasn't the Taj Mahal. Everybody starts somewhere, so I recommend starting as cheap and as small as you can, without being too small, to make sure you can attract as many people as possible to become tenants.

Two-bedrooms are great and three-bedrooms are better, but make sure your three-bedroom home is in an affordable range. Ideally, you want to be able to rent it as the lowest three-bedroom price on the market, allowing you to keep it occupied all of the time.

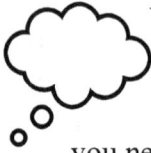

Reflection: Defining Your Ideal Tenant Profile

Before you buy any property, you need to clearly understand who will want to live there. This isn't about discrimination—it's about smart market positioning to ensure your property rents quickly and consistently.

What's the demographic profile of your target area? Drive around your potential investment neighborhoods at different times of day. Who do you see? Young professionals heading to work? Families with kids playing in yards? College students? Retirees? The existing residents will tell you a lot about who might rent your property.

What does your local rental market demand? Research rental listings in your area. What size properties rent fastest? What price points have the most competition among renters? Are there more people looking for one-bedrooms or three-bedrooms? This data should influence your property choice.

How does location affect your tenant pool? Map out what's within a 5-mile radius of potential properties. Schools, hospitals, universities, major employers, public transportation? Each of these attracts different types of tenants with different needs and budgets.

What's the sweet spot for rental demand?
Generally, properties that appeal to the broadest
range of tenants rent fastest. A two- or three-
bedroom house in an affordable price range will
typically have more potential renters than a luxury
four-bedroom or a tiny studio. Where's that sweet
spot in your market?

**Can your target tenants actually afford
your property?** If you're targeting young
professionals, research average salaries in your area.
If you're near a university, find out typical student
housing budgets. Make sure your rental price aligns
with what your target market can realistically pay.

**What are the lifestyle needs of your target
tenants?** Families need safe neighborhoods and
good schools. Young professionals might prioritize
commute times and nightlife. Students care about
proximity to campus and affordability. How well
does your potential property serve these needs?

How stable is your target tenant group?
Some tenants are more likely to stay long-term
(families, established professionals) while others are
transient (students, job transferees). What level of
turnover are you comfortable managing? How does
this affect your investment strategy?

What's your competitive advantage? If
you're targeting the same demographic as every

other landlord in the area, what will make tenants choose your property? Better price? Better amenities? Better location? Better service? You need something that sets you apart.

Remember, the goal isn't to find the perfect tenant—it's to buy a property that appeals to a large pool of qualified potential tenants. The broader your appeal (within your target market), the faster your property will rent and the more leverage you'll have in choosing good tenants.

Chapter 15

Leave Your Emotions Behind

This cannot be stressed enough: NO EMOTIONS ALLOWED! I mean it, none. This is a business decision, an investment. You can't get caught up in irrelevant details. I don't care if it has your favorite color carpet, I don't care if they painted a mural on the wall that's exactly what you like or you're into. It doesn't matter.

I don't care if it's in the neighborhood you've always wanted to move into, or you always thought it was cute, or you drove by it every day and you just loved the front porch. None of that matters because when you're making a purchase offer, it is all about business.

Don't Let Dislikes Cloud Your Judgment Either

On the flip side, make sure you aren't making any decisions based on cosmetic aspects that you *don't* like, such as the colors of the walls, carpet, countertops, or even the cabinets themselves. I've changed out all of that, and it's not that expensive to do.

For instance, if you decide the cabinets are too dark for your liking but the base is nice and sturdy, you can have a cabinetmaker put new doors and hardware on for an inexpensive price, and voilà—they look brand new. Lighting is also inexpensive to change out, and home improvement stores have great prices on nice-looking fixtures.

Don't ever pass up a profitable rental property just because the cosmetics don't suit your taste. If the structure of the property is good, see what you can do to change out the colors and other options that would better attract tenants. It may not be as expensive as you think. You don't have to make it look like a home decorator show either—just don't get wrapped up in your personal preferences.

Business Decisions Only

Remember, if we're going to be High Heels Landlords, we're going to have to make a profit. We're going to have to show that we can do this. Decisions need to be business-based, not based on emotions.

I know people who have bought entire blocks of homes because they've always liked that street or they've always wanted to live there. That's not smart. Leave your emotions behind.

And don't ever buy a house on a whim. Go home, sleep on it, think about it, pray about it—do what you need to do to make sure it is the right business decision for you.

Again, this is a business, so leave the emotions out. It's like hiring and firing someone. It's part of the job. Leave the emotions at home.

Reflection: Mastering Your Emotional Triggers

Separating emotions from business decisions is one of the hardest skills to master in real estate investing, but it's absolutely critical for success. Let's identify where you might be vulnerable.

What are your emotional triggers when looking at properties? Do you get excited about beautiful kitchens? Charming architectural details? Properties in "nice" neighborhoods? Or do you get turned off by outdated décor, strange paint colors, or older fixtures? Make a list of what emotionally attracts or repels you so you can recognize when these feelings are influencing your judgment.

How do you typically make major purchase decisions? Think about buying your car, your home, or other big-ticket items. Are you an impulse buyer who falls in love and buys immediately? Or do you agonize over decisions for weeks? Understanding your natural decision-making style will help you create systems to keep yourself objective.

What's your strategy for taking emotion out of the equation? Some investors bring a trusted advisor to property viewings. Others use strict checklists and won't deviate from their criteria. Some take photos and review them later when they're not standing in the property. What system will work for your personality?

How will you handle "dream property syndrome"? Every investor encounters a property that seems perfect—great location, beautiful features, everything they've ever wanted. But if the numbers don't work, you have to walk away. How will you remind yourself that there will always be another property?

What's your plan for the "ugly duckling" dilemma? Sometimes the best investment properties are the ones that look terrible but have great bones. Can you see past hideous wallpaper and outdated fixtures to evaluate the true potential? How will you train yourself to focus on structure, location, and numbers rather than aesthetics?

Who's your voice of reason? Every investor needs someone who can talk them out of emotional decisions or encourage them when they're hesitating over a good deal for the wrong reasons. Who in your life can fill this role? Your spouse? A mentor? An experienced investor friend?

How will you handle buyer's remorse or FOMO? After you walk away from a property for business reasons, you might second-guess yourself. Or after you make an offer, you might panic and want to back out. What's your plan for managing these normal but potentially destructive emotions?

What mantras or reminders will keep you focused? Some investors have phrases they repeat: "Buy with my calculator, not my heart," or "I'm buying an investment, not a home." What words will snap you back to business mode when emotions start taking over?

Remember, the properties that make you feel emotional—either positive or negative—are often the ones where you're most likely to make poor business decisions. The best investment properties might be the ones that make you feel absolutely nothing at all.

Chapter 16

The Makings of a High Heels Landlord

Whether or not you wear high heels is irrelevant at this point. What *does* matter is your independence. Real estate can provide that, as well as give you some financial stability and confidence.

So to wrap things up and recap: make sure you know what you want property-wise, and that you want it for all the right reasons. Also, consider your sources for advice (lots of people gave you advice on becoming a new parent, right?) before deciding whether or not to follow it.

Make sure you do all your necessary homework and get your finances in order before purchasing a property. Get the necessary advice if you are going to incorporate, and decide on your exit strategy upfront before making any moves.

Hire a Realtor® to help you with your purchase, preferably one with investment expertise who owns his or her own rental properties. Have a checklist of your needs and wants for your purchase, and don't be afraid to offend others with your offers. Remember, this is a business investment. Treat it as such.

Additionally, price is everything, and nothing else matters! It's also important to understand what amenities are important and add to the value of your rental. Which ones are needs and which ones are wants?

If you have little to no experience in real estate, don't get into large multi-family properties right away. Start on a smaller scale instead. There's always time to grow and expand once you have some experience.

Finally, develop a good idea of what type of tenant will be renting the property you are trying to purchase, and leave your emotions out of it. This is a business decision, so always treat it like one.

If you follow these rules, you will be on your way to becoming a true High Heels Landlord.

Reflection: Your Action Plan for Success

Congratulations! You've learned the fundamentals of real estate investing. But knowledge without action is just entertainment. It's time to turn everything you've learned into a concrete plan for building your financial independence.

What's your very first step? Will you start by researching your local market, getting your finances in order, or finding an experienced Realtor®? Don't try to do everything at once.

What's the one thing you'll do this week to move closer to your first investment property?

How will you measure your progress? Success in real estate doesn't happen overnight. How will you track your journey? Will you set goals for when you want to buy your first property? How many properties you want to own in five years? What your target monthly income should be? Write down specific, measurable goals.

What's your learning plan? This book is just the beginning. Will you take a real estate course? Join a local real estate investment group? Find a mentor? Continue reading books and listening to podcasts? How will you keep expanding your knowledge?

Who's going to hold you accountable? Real estate investing can be scary, and it's easy to make excuses and delay taking action. Who in your life will encourage you to move forward when you're feeling uncertain? Who will celebrate your successes with you?

What fears do you need to overcome? Be honest about what's holding you back. Are you worried about making mistakes? Concerned about dealing with tenants? Afraid of taking on debt? Identify your fears so you can address them head-on rather than let them paralyze you.

How will you stay motivated during tough times? Every real estate investor faces challenges—difficult tenants, unexpected repairs, market downturns. What will keep you going when things get hard? Remember your "why" from the beginning of this book and keep it front and center.

What does success look like for you personally? Financial independence means different things to different people. Some want to replace their job income, others want to fund their children's education, and still others want a comfortable retirement. Paint a clear picture of what success looks like for your life specifically.

When will you take action? The best time to start investing in real estate was yesterday. The second-best time is today. What's your timeline for taking your first concrete step? Don't let "someday" become never.

Remember, every successful real estate investor started exactly where you are right now—with knowledge, determination, and a willingness to take that first scary step. You have everything you need to succeed. The only question is: when will you begin?

Your journey to becoming a High Heels Landlord starts with a single step. Take it today.

Conclusion

As with any serious investment purchase, you should always surround yourself with trusted advisors. Some of the best decisions I have made have been with the help of advisors like these.

Advisors you may want to seek as you journey on the road to becoming a High Heels Landlord include: a qualified CPA who knows the ins and outs of rental properties, a real estate attorney who can help you review purchase and sales contracts, a Realtor® (if you are not one), and an experienced investor to bounce ideas off of.

It also helps if you know someone who will provide private financing so you don't have to go to lending institutions for your mortgages. This will not only save you the hassle of dealing with traditional lenders, but it can also save you money on the overall fees they charge.

There is no price you can put on good, sound advice, which can come from any of these sources listed above. That makes having this group of advisors worth their weight in gold.

Good luck on your journey to becoming a High Heels Landlord! God bless.

www.ingramcontent.com/pod-product-compliance
Lightning Source LLC
Chambersburg PA
CBHW062005200326
41519CB00017B/4678